W9-ANW-774

Presented to:

We will shout for joy when you are victorious and will lift up our banners in the name of our God. May the LORD grant all your requests.

PSALM 20:5

Presented by:

Date:

Celebrate the Graduate

★

Heartwarming Stories, Inspirational Sayings, and Loving Expressions to Honor a Special Graduate

Celebrate the Graduate:
Heartwarming Stories, Inspirational Sayings, and Loving Expressions to Honor a Special Graduate

ISBN 1-59379-058-9

Published by White Stone Books
P.O. Box 2835
Lakeland, Florida 33806

Manuscript written and compiled by SnapdragonGroup℠ Editorial Services

Contents

All our life is a celebration for us; we are convinced,
in fact, that God is always everywhere.
We sing while we work; we pray while we
carry out all life's other occupations.

Clement of Alexandria
Early Greek Theologian
Unknown-215 A.D.

Introduction

Congratulations! Your big day has finally come and you are about to embark on your own "great adventure"! You're a living, breathing, yet-to-be-written success story, and you've got the diploma to prove it. Expect blessings, expect challenges, expect the unexpected. And, don't let anyone rain on your parade.

Consider this book a tool to be used on your journey through life. Each story, poem, quote, scripture, affirmation, reflection, and challenge has been added to encourage you to become the personal success God created you to be. As you embark on your journey, our prayer is that you will have every confidence that comes from your significant accomplishment and great hope for a bright future.

It takes courage to live—courage and strength and hope and humor.

JEROME P. FLEISHMAN

Success Is Courage and Strength

Having thus chosen our course, let us renew our trust in God and go forward without fear.

Abraham Lincoln
1809-1865
American President 1861-1865

Now that you've graduated, you're well on your way down the road to success. Keep in mind, however, that success is both a destination and a lifelong journey. Conquer your fears—one at a time—by placing your confidence in God and holding on to your courage. Don't let the uncertainties of life hold you back from your dreams.

Be bold and strong!
Banish fear and doubt!
For remember, the LORD your God
is with you wherever you go.

JOSHUA 1:9 TLB

I do not ask to walk smooth paths
Nor bear an easy load,
I pray for strength and fortitude
To climb the rock-strewn road.
Give me such courage I can scale
The hardest peaks alone,
And transform every stumbling block
Into a stepping-stone.

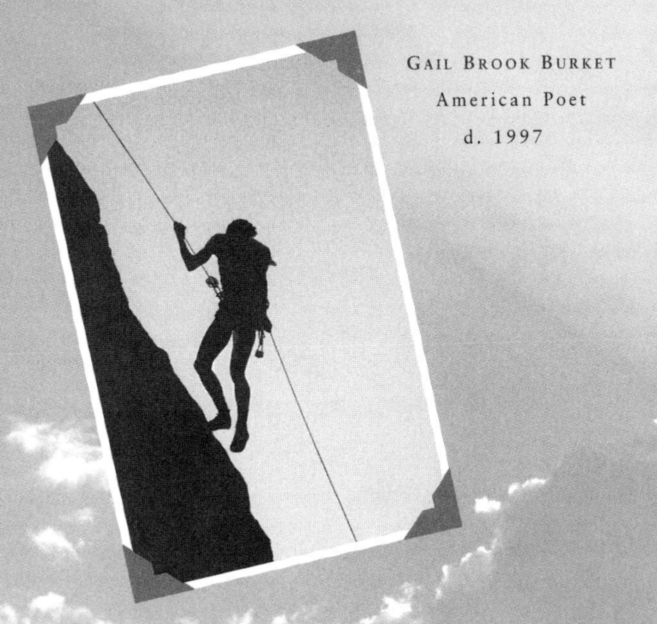

GAIL BROOK BURKET
American Poet
d. 1997

Courage and Strength

- Face small challenges and overcome them. For instance, if you're shy by nature, be the first to speak to people as they approach you in a public setting. Smile, make eye contact, and simply say hello. You'll find a lot of smiles coming back at you!

- Learn to be effective on the telephone by speaking clearly and in an upbeat tone. Before you make the call, have in front of you the name, number, and a small note concerning the reason for the call.

- Learn to deliver a strong and confident handshake by practicing on friends and family members.

- The apostle Paul said, "I can do all things through Christ who strengthens me" (Philippians 4:13 NKJV). Joel 3:10 KJV instructs, "Let the weak say, 'I am strong.'" The next time you feel weary or overwhelmed, practice making these statements yourself, and trust in God's strength. You really can do everything you need to do when He is empowering you!

- Post encouraging scriptures or favorite quotes where you will see them often—on a mirror, the refrigerator, or the dashboard of your car.

- Read books that will motivate you to reach beyond yourself and become a better person. Try the following: *I Dare You* by William Danforth, *How to Win Friends and Influence People* by Dale Carnegie, and *See You at the Top* by Zig Ziglar.

Let no one nor anything stand between you and the difficult task, let nothing deny you this rich chance to gain strength by adversity, confidence by mastery, success by deserving it. Do it better each time. Do it better than anyone else can do it. I know this sounds old-fashioned. It is, but it has built the world.

HARLOW H. CURTICE
1950s General Motors Executive

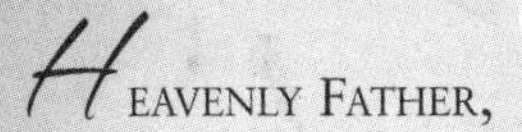

Heavenly Father,

Thank You for being with me every day of my life. You've given me strength for long hours of study, understanding and insight for tackling difficult assignments, and confidence and calm for those stomach-turning exams.

Now I'm facing a whole new reality—life after school—and I need Your guidance for the journey ahead. Once again I'm asking for strength and courage to face my future and find and conquer the destiny to which You've called me.

Amen.

A Certain Smile

I had been crying for close to an hour when a friend called. I gasped a few words into the phone. "I'm all right ... sniff ... I'm just so tired ... sniff ... overwhelmed. I can't think ... sniff, sniff ... but I'll be fine ... really ... I just need to get some sleep and try to decide what to do," I choked. My college buddy was nearly ten years younger than I, and male. He couldn't possibly understand what going to school, raising a child alone, and trying to work all at the same time meant.

I have never been worth much when I let myself get beyond the point of exhaustion, and I was more than tired that night. There were baskets of laundry in the living room, dishes in the sink, and the dryer was buzzing. My daughter was sobbing in her room after I had told her I couldn't help with a science project because my term paper was due at 7:30 in the morning, and she had just spilled her drink all over my notes! The landlord had called wanting to be paid, and once again the child support for that month had not come. To top it all off, I had a flat tire.

What a mess. And there I was—a sophomore in college; too far in to drop out, too far from the finish line to imagine ever crossing it.

Twenty minutes later the vice president of the college and

two professors were at my door. I was shocked and horrified at the same time. "May we come in?" they asked politely.

"Oh, I ... oh, it is such a mess in here, I ... did Jeff call you? ... I am so sorry! ... I told him I was fine ... I am ... really ... I am so embarrassed ..." I stammered, wishing I could disappear into the floor.

"We didn't come to see your house; we came to see you," Dr. Wright said, gently putting his hand on my shoulder. We know how hard this is for you. We just wanted to stop by and encourage you and see if we could help in any way."

Such a nice man, I thought between moments of panic and embarrassment.

"Oh no! I'm ... just really overly tired—a little overwhelmed. But honestly, I'll be fine tomorrow. He shouldn't have called you—really," I stammered.

"Darla is in my entrepreneur class," Dr. Wright said, as he nodded to his companions to follow him inside. "I have to tell you how impressed I am with your comments and participation, Darla. You really add to the class and give such insightful perspectives."

"Thank you," I offered weakly. I was surprised he even took notice I was in his class since I wasn't even a business major.

"Darla, you're going to be fine. You're going to make it!" Dr. Wright continued. "I know you're tired, but I know you have what it takes to pull this off."

I smiled a little and looked up to meet his gaze.

"When you graduate, do you know who hands you your diploma? ... I do," he said smiling. "I'm going to be there the day you graduate—and I'm going to look right at you when I call your name and smile. At that moment, you and I will be remembering this day when you wanted to give it all up—but didn't."

There was such surety in his voice that I couldn't help but believe him.

I did survive that night, finished my term paper, helped with the science project, and did the laundry and dishes. Some friends even stopped by and "happened to have" a tire for my car with them!

"Thank You, Lord," I prayed, "for the courage and strength to keep going until I reach my dreams."

Two years later, Dr. Hal Wright called out my name, and faithful to his word, he turned, we smiled that smile, and he handed me my diploma. I will never forget that man or the fact that he had faith in me even when I couldn't believe in myself. Faith is an amazing tool. It is the ability to see beyond your circumstances to the possibilities—that flicker of hope that turns everything around.[1]

★

Courage and Strength

Because Christ strengthens me, I have the grace to do everything I need to do today. I am strong and courageous because my Father has promised to go with me and fight for me. I strive to please Him, because when I do, He causes even my enemies to be at peace with me! I have nothing to fear with Him by my side. Now that I've graduated, I determine to take the first courageous steps toward success—the fulfillment of God's perfect will for my life.

Far better it is to dare mighty things,

to win glorious triumphs,

even though checkered by failure,

than to take rank with those poor spirits

who neither enjoy much nor suffer much

because they live in the gray twilight

that knows no victory nor defeat.

THEODORE ROOSEVELT
1858-1919
American President 1901-1909

No one ever became wise by chance.

Lucius Annaeus Seneca

Roman Playwright

5 B.C.-65 A.D

Success Is Wisdom and Knowledge

Knowledge is horizontal.
Wisdom is vertical—
it comes down from above.

BILLY GRAHAM
Beloved American Evangelist

Knowledge and understanding are the hallmarks of a great education.
Now that you've graduated, you'll need to apply wisdom to what you've learned.
Your future success depends on it.

If any of you lacks wisdom,
he should ask God, who gives generously
to all without finding fault,
and it will be given to him.

JAMES 1:5

Don't expect wisdom to come into your life like
great chunks of rock on a conveyor belt. It isn't like that.
It's not splashy and bold ... nor is it dispensed like a prescription across a counter. Wisdom comes privately
from God as a by-product of right decisions, godly reactions, and the application of spiritual principles to daily circumstances. Wisdom comes ... not from trying to do great things for God but more from being faithful to the small, obscure tasks few people ever see.

CHARLES SWINDOLL
American Author and Bible Teacher

Wisdom and Knowledge

- Get in the habit of asking questions of the people you know who are experts in your areas of interest.
- Keep a journal to jot down interesting information and facts about your areas of interest as you come across them.
- Learn from the experience of others in your field. Take time to watch them work. Pay attention to the processes they have developed to get things done.
- Join a professional organization that can offer tips and updates in your professional field.
- Ask God to give you wisdom and insight regarding the difficult people in your life. Ask Him to help you understand what makes them tick. Since He created them, He knows the most productive way for you to interact with them.
- Read one chapter each day from the book of Proverbs in the Bible. Interestingly, there are thirty-one wisdom-filled chapters in this book, one for each day of the month. Determine to put into practice what you read each day.

Wisdom is the right use of knowledge.

CHARLES SPURGEON
Greatest British Preacher of His Time
1834-1892

Wisdom is as good as an inheritance, an advantage to those who see the sun.

ECCLESIASTES 7:11 NRSV

Heavenly Father,

I've worked so hard and learned so much. Sometimes it feels overwhelming. Just knowing how to apply all I've learned is going to take a lot of wisdom. For that I'm depending on You. I know my own wisdom is often tainted by misconceptions and bias—but Your wisdom, Lord, is pure and holy and eternal.

I'll be coming to You often, asking for so much. I'm glad Your patience is perfect and Your generosity is greater than I could ever think or imagine. I thank You in advance for helping me use all that I've learned in order to become all that You've created me to be and to achieve real success.

Amen.

Win-Win Wisdom

While rocking my first baby one night, my mind drifted back to my high school graduation. It didn't seem possible that so much time had passed. I remembered so vividly memorizing Robert Frost's poem "The Road Not Taken" my senior year in English:

Two roads diverged in a yellow wood,

And sorry I could not travel both

And be one traveler, long I stood

And looked down one as far as I could. …

And I—took the one less traveled by

And that has made all the difference.

My graduation did lead me down a road less traveled, but not one I would have chosen voluntarily. A few short months after graduation, my parents ended their twenty-year marriage. They thought they were saving their kids the pain of divorce by waiting until we were almost grown. Not true!

The news sent me into a tailspin. I was hurt, confused, and without direction. Wasn't this supposed to be the happiest time of my life? I had planned on entering college that fall, but my heart just wasn't in it. All through high school, I had believed that God had a special plan for my life, but now I wasn't sure. I felt paralyzed.

I wanted to attend college. I had earned scholarships in piano and wanted to major in church music. How-ever, part of me felt like I would be deserting my younger sisters if I left home. As is typical of an oldest child, I also felt like my mother desperately needed my help and support.

Eventually, I shared my dilemma with my mother and asked her to pray with me. I wanted clear assur-ance about what to do with my life. In her wisdom, Mom told me that she couldn't choose what road was best for me, but she did encourage me to get on with my life—whatever that was!

To reassure me, my wise mother read Isaiah 42:16 to me, "I will lead the blind by ways they have not known, along unfamiliar paths I will guide them; I will turn the darkness into light before them and make the rough places smooth. These are the things I will do; I will not forsake them."

Then she said, "When you realize how much God loves you, you'll come to know that when you make what you determine to be the 'right' decision and it's God's way for you, then God will bless it. And when you make a decision that you think is right, but it doesn't work out to be God's best path for you, He will redeem it. Either way, you have nothing to fear because your loving Father has His hand on you."

I went away to college that fall, but I was so unhappy that

I came back home. My decision haunted me. Was I only running away, or had God's Spirit really led me to quit? Either way, my mother's wisdom sustained me, and the Lord did redeem my choice.

A few months later, I was offered a well-paying position as assistant to the worship director at a large church in Virginia Beach. I'd chosen the less-traveled road and landed a job I thought would require four years of college—a job that brought me great fulfillment for many years and landed me right in the middle of God's will.

I look back now to that difficult time, and it has become the defining moment of what I remember most about graduating from high school.

As I peacefully rocked my newborn son, I whispered, "Sweet baby boy, you've nothing to fear in life because your Heavenly Father loves and cares for you. May you come to know that He'll bless your wise decisions and redeem your foolish ones—just like He did for your mommy."[2]

★

Wisdom and Knowledge

Because I seek wisdom from God, I am walking forward into my future with confidence. I am expecting opportunities in abundance and celebrate the gift of wisdom God gives me to make the most of those opportunities. I am determined to succeed by pleasing God and living my life in harmony with His perfect will.

Be sure of the foundation of your life.

Know why you live as you do.

Be ready to give a reason for it.

Do not, in such a matter as life,

build an opinion or custom on what you guess is true.

Make it a matter of certainty.

THOMAS STARR KING

American Lecturer and Orator

1824-1864

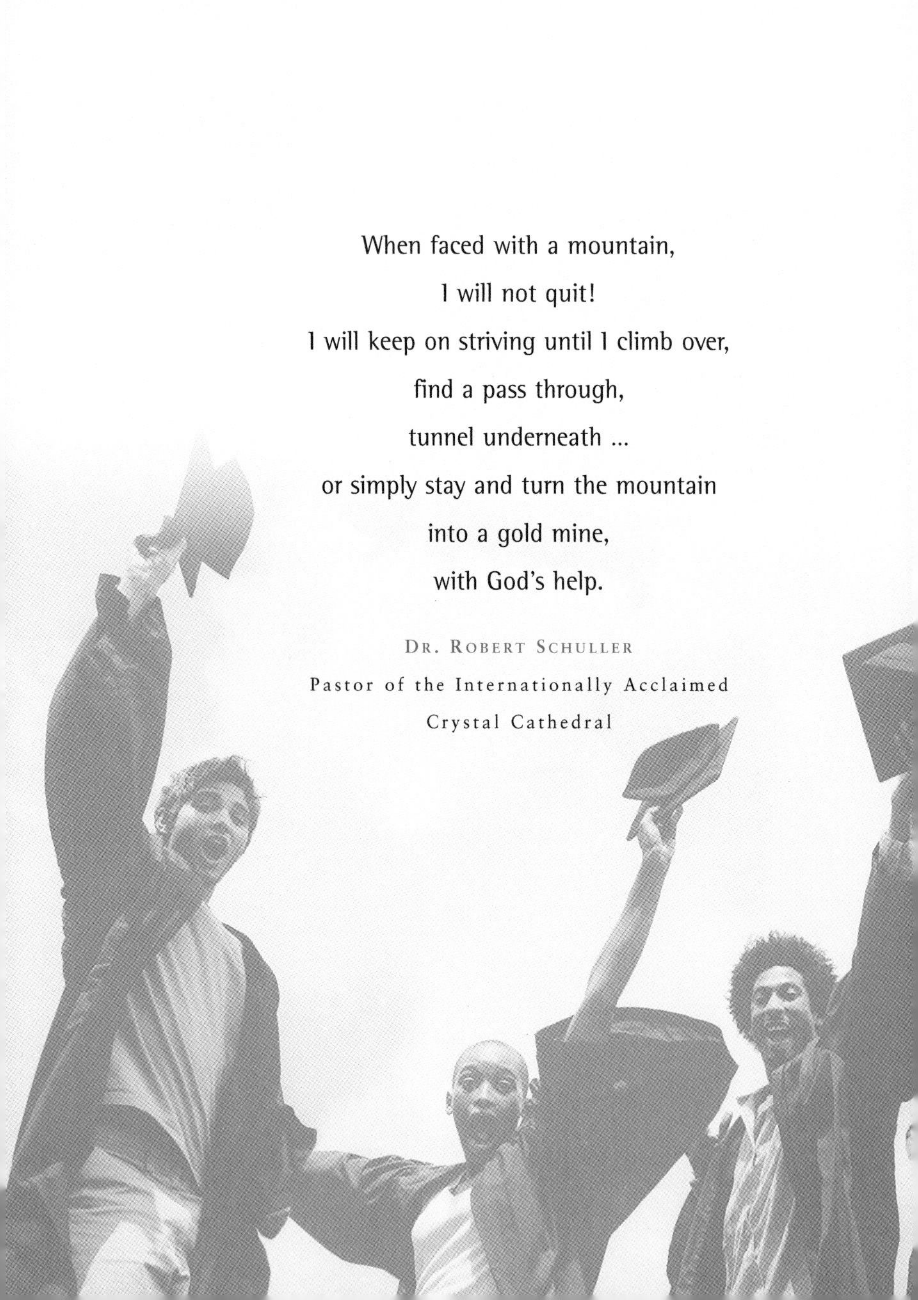

When faced with a mountain,
I will not quit!
I will keep on striving until I climb over,
find a pass through,
tunnel underneath ...
or simply stay and turn the mountain
into a gold mine,
with God's help.

Dr. Robert Schuller
Pastor of the Internationally Acclaimed
Crystal Cathedral

Success Is Determination and Diligence

Avoid the last-minute rush; do it yesterday.

AUTHOR UNKNOWN

Far more people make it to Graduation Day because of determination and diligence than talent and intelligence. The road to success is no different. It is conquered by putting one foot in front of another ... and another ... and another ... and another.

Let us not grow weary in doing what is right, for we will reap at harvest-time, if we do not give up.

GALATIANS 6:9 NRSV

No one ever attains very eminent success
by simply doing what is required of him;
it is the amount and excellence
of what is over and above the required
that determines the greatness
of ultimate distinction.

CHARLES KENDALL ADAMS
American Educator
1835-1902

Determination and Diligence

- Plan small rewards for yourself to celebrate tasks completed. This might be an evening out with friends, a bike ride with the wind in your face, or even an ice-cream cone.

- Set long-term (one-, five-, ten-year) and short-term (daily, weekly, monthly) goals to achieve your objectives. When you tackle one small goal at a time, eventually you will find yourself making headway and achieving great things.

- Set a "minimum daily requirement" for those inevitable days when you are not able to accomplish your regular, daily goals. If you can complete just one thing, you will still be gaining ground.

- Read the amazing story of how determination and diligence paid off in the life of Joseph in Genesis 37, 39-45.

- To stay motivated, read in the book of Proverbs about how God has promised to bless the diligent: Proverbs 10:4; 12:24, 27; 13:4; 21:5.

- Never, ever give up!

- Seek God about His plan for your life. Write it down and refer to it often. (See Habakkuk 2:2-3 KJV.) It is much easier to weather the storms of life when you know you are on God's path for you, for it is then that you can trust Him to help you overcome.

The difference between the impossible and the possible lies in a person's determination.

TOMMY LASORDA
One of the Most Passionate and Successful Managers in Baseball History

The desires of the diligent are fully satisfied.

PROVERBS 13:4

HEAVENLY FATHER,

I LIKE THE FEELING OF THIS DAY—BEING ABLE TO LOOK BACK AT ALL MY HARD WORK AND REJOICE IN WHAT I'VE ACCOMPLISHED WITH YOUR HELP. I'D LIKE TO HAVE THAT FEELING AGAIN ON THE DAY MY LIFE ENDS AND I STAND BEFORE YOU IN ETERNITY.

HELP ME NOT TO LOSE SIGHT OF MY DREAMS, LORD. WHEN I'M WEAK, LEND ME YOUR STRENGTH. WHEN I'M TIRED, LEND ME YOUR ENERGY. WHEN I'M LACKING MOTIVATION, LEND ME YOUR ZEAL. I WANT THE KIND OF SUCCESS THAT HAS ETERNAL BENEFITS, THE KIND OF SUCCESS THAT PLEASES YOU.

I'VE WORKED HARD AND WITH GREAT DETERMINA-TION TO GET TO THIS DAY. AFTER I'VE RESTED FOR A WHILE, REGAINED MY SANITY, RENEWED MY RE-SOURCES, GIVE ME THE KICK I NEED TO GET UP AND GO BACK TO WORK. HELP ME TO LIVE MY LIFE IN A WAY THAT WOULD ADD MEANING AND PURPOSE TO EACH DAY.

AMEN.

When the Family Genes Kicked In

At the age of eighteen, the lure of a "white picket fence" and the dream of living "happily ever after" stole my heart and clouded my reasoning. Both of my parents were well-educated and encouraged me to attend college and get a teaching credential. But I didn't realize that I had inherited my parents' love of learning or that I would someday value an education. Eventually, I would learn these truths the hard way. Instead, I eloped my freshman year and dropped out of college.

Ten years later I was a single mom with three small children. My ex-husband had destroyed my self-image. My one semester of high school typing and a little file clerk experience were the only job skills I had to support my family. How would I ever manage financially? Fortunately, I found a job that paid enough for the kids and me to live on, but as careful as I was, making ends meet was still difficult.

In spite of everything, I was smart enough to realize my negative attitude about myself could have long-lasting, harmful effects on my children. I was determined not to let that happen. Could I change? What if my parents had been right all along? Maybe I did need a college education. If I could go back to school, maybe I wouldn't feel so inadequate. There were many things to consider—family and work, time and money. Could I juggle everything without becoming exhausted or discouraged? Would I have what it takes to complete such a long undertaking?

I've heard it said that "the journey of a thousand miles begins with the first step." I decided to take that step by enrolling in a night-school class. I knew I could study on my lunch hour and late into the night after the children were in bed. That's all the time I had. I hoped it would be enough.

My good grades did not come easily, but they were motivation to continue each semester on the long journey for my college degree. The family genes kicked in, and as I pursued my education, I felt a little better about myself every day.

A few years later I remarried, and in so doing created a blended family with seven children. I continued taking one or two classes each semester until the last child had left home. I prayed hard and often about finishing up my degree and felt convinced God was giving me the go-ahead. I no longer needed a degree for a better job. By now I was loved and admired by my husband, and I had long since ceased to think of myself as incapable. But within my heart was that burning desire to get a degree—to complete the journey I had begun so many years ago. I decided to attend college full time.

It didn't matter that I was older than my professors or that my classmates couldn't believe I was in college for the love of learning and not just to prepare for a career. Every morning I looked forward to my day on campus. It was a thrill I can't explain. I loved it! Evenings and weekends found me with my nose in a book. Whatever social life I had was only permissible if I was caught up on my studying.

Only a few more classes remained when a dark cloud appeared on the horizon. It was not one I could change. About the time I decided to attend college full time, my elderly mother's health took a turn for the worse. So each day after school, I would drive to her house and take care of her needs and then drive home to study. Twenty-four hours before I began my last semester, she passed away. Even though she didn't live to see me graduate, I know she was proud that I had returned to school to complete my degree.

On May 26, 1990, when my name was called to come forward and receive my diploma, words of inadequacy and low self-esteem did not come forward with me. With God's help, they had been defeated by a woman who had just completed a long and difficult journey.[3]

★

Determination and Diligence

I am applying myself to God's plan for my life with diligence and determination. I am trusting God to take my offering and make of it eternal success—a life that is profitable for the kingdom of God. And I thank God for helping me stand firm and never quit!

You can do what you want to do,
accomplish what you want to accomplish,
attain any reasonable objective you may have in mind—not all of a
sudden, perhaps not in one swift
and sweeping act of achievement—
but you can do it gradually,
day by day and play by play,
if you want to do it,
if you work to do it,
over a sufficiently long period of time.

William E. Holler
Chevrolet Executive, Author, and Motivational Speaker
1889-1969

Faithfulness in little things
is a big thing.

SAINT JOHN CHRYSOSTOM
Archbishop and Patriarch of Constantinople
347-407

Success Is Faithfulness and Truth

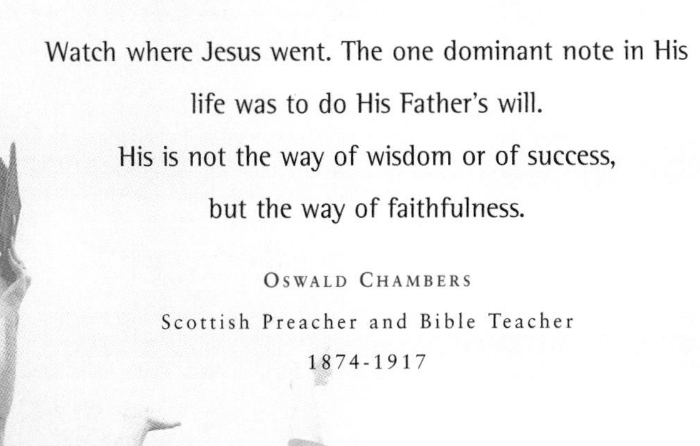

Watch where Jesus went. The one dominant note in His life was to do His Father's will. His is not the way of wisdom or of success, but the way of faithfulness.

OSWALD CHAMBERS
Scottish Preacher and Bible Teacher
1874-1917

Your Graduation Day would not have come
if it weren't for your faithful commitment
to your education.
And if you were also committed to the truth,
you know that you've gained as much as
possible from your education.
Your future success depends on how well you
continue to be faithful and truthful.
Don't settle for anything less.

Buy the truth and do not sell it; get wisdom, discipline and understanding.

PROVERBS 23:23

Seek the truth

Listen to the truth

Teach the truth

Love the truth

Abide by the truth

And defend the truth

Unto death.

John Huss
Czech Religious Reformer
1369-1415

Faithfulness and Truth

- Be a person of your word.
- Be on time–all the time.
- Finish what you start. Pace yourself well.
- Always do your best, even when no one is looking. God, who sees your faithfulness in secret, will reward you openly. (See Matthew 6:4 and Ephesians 6:5-8.)
- Hook up with others who set a high standard. Be a part of what they are doing and learn.
- Read God's promises of how He will reward your faithfulness: Psalm 18:25; 31:23; 37:28; 97:10; 101:6; Proverbs 2:8; 28:20.
- Let the Word of God be your standard. Culture and trends constantly change, but God's truth and principles never change.

The best advice I can give to any young man or young woman upon graduation from school can be summed up in exactly eight words, and they are—be honest with yourself and tell the truth.

JAMES A. FARLEY

Politician, Businessman, and Postmaster General under President Franklin Roosevelt

1888-1976

Heavenly Father,

The older I become the more I'm exposed to society's tendency to stretch, ignore, avoid, and bend the truth. Far from condemning it, I'm told to embrace "situation ethics." And even if I am truthful, what's to say that other people will be truthful with me?

I'm so glad, Lord, that You don't change with the circumstances. You represent absolute truth. I believe that when I'm vitally connected to You, I, too, will be able to identify the truth and walk in it. I'll also be able to make it an unwavering filter for my thoughts, words, and attitudes.

Help me throughout my life to walk with You in absolute truth.

Amen.

Returning the Favor

Dear Mom and Dad,

Tomorrow I graduate from high school. The day after that I will officially enter the adult world, and life as I know it will end. Although I've been waiting for this day since I realized there was an end to first grade, I can admit—at least on paper—that I'm sort of "excitedly terrified" by what lies ahead.

I've been making my college wish list for more than a year. I've shopped till I dropped for sheets, storage boxes, bookshelves, computer software, and the "right" clothes. I've set out my four-year plan, which will probably change in six months, and stuffed suitcases with pieces of home.

The real question is: Am I ready for life? Report cards and transcripts show what I learned in twelve years of school, or at least what I passed. But what about the real world? Will I be a responsible citizen and a good parent or employee? Will I be a friend someone will be proud to claim? Do I have what it takes to succeed? My first thought is, *Of course not! I'm just a kid!*

But then I started thinking about all you've taught me. You never once said, "Now I'm going to teach you about character or integrity or honesty or responsibility." You just lived them before me. You taught me to be humble when I was right and apologetic when I was wrong.

You also taught me that with privilege comes responsibility and that nothing in life is free. That summer we bought my American saddle-bred mare, I pictured riding all day every day. Was I wrong! There was a barn stall to be cleaned, fences to be painted, hay to be stacked, and water tanks to be filled.

But you also taught me how to rest and have fun. My childhood wasn't all work and no play. I remember lazy summer days playing outside or taking a nap or reading a book on Sunday after church. You taught me to love life!

You also taught me that choices and consequences always go hand in hand. Mom, do you remember the day I went grocery shopping with you, and from the minute we pulled into the parking lot, I fussed and whined about getting my way? What was I thinking? Even though we'd only gone down half the aisles, you pushed the cart to the front of the store, asked the clerk if you could leave it there, and said you'd be back shortly. Then you took me by the hand and we walked to the car in silence. I had only one thought: *I am so busted!*

When Dad asked why we were home so early and with no groceries, you said I could explain. I found out just how much saddle soap and "elbow grease" it takes to polish four saddles.

You taught me to be kind to people, animals, and the

environment. You taught me that it's okay to be afraid, but it's not okay to stay afraid. You taught me not to be judgmental because there is always one more fact I don't know. You taught me that honesty is the best policy no matter what. You taught me so many things, I think I could fill a book with your wisdom.

I'd like to say that I have always done as you advised, that I've never brought you shame or embarrassment, but you also taught me to tell the truth.

And the truth, Mom and Dad, is that I want to say thank you, not only for sacrificing so I can go to college, but for all you've done in preparing me for this day. You've given me a solid foundation and been a great example.

Now it's my turn to do the same, learning from my mistakes as I go. Hopefully, Dad, I'll remember the words you always said with a wink, "Of course you're allowed a mistake. Just don't make the same one twice." My response was always, "I'll do my best."

And I will, Mom and Dad, not only to make you proud of me, but also to be the kind of person who will, hopefully, get a letter like this from her own child someday.

Lovingly,

Your daughter[4]

★

Faithfulness and Truth

God's Word of Truth says that the faithful abound with blessings, so I commit to be a faithful servant of God. Because I do this, the Lord promises to preserve me, to keep His eyes on me continually, and to dwell with me. His truth is my standard, and as I faithfully conduct myself according to it, my Father is able to say, "Well done, good and faithful servant."

Soak and soak and soak continually in the one great truth
of which you have had a vision;
take it to bed with you,
sleep with it, rise up in the morning with it,
continually bring your imagination into captivity to it,
and slowly and surely as the months and years go by,
God will make you one of his specialists
in that particular truth.

OSWALD CHAMBERS
Scottish Preacher and Bible Teacher
1874-1917

One of the most important ways to manifest integrity is to be loyal to those who are not present. In doing so, we build the trust of those who are present.

STEPHEN R. COVEY
American Author and Motivational Speaker

Success Is Integrity and Industry

Success in life depends upon the three I's: integrity, intelligence, and industry.

CHARLES STOCKARD
American Psychologist
1879-1939

Now that you've graduated, you will find that the challenges to your integrity may not be as clear-cut as they were while you were in school, but the principle is the same—do the right thing.

The desires of good people lead straight to the best, but wicked ambition ends in angry frustration.

PROVERBS 11:23 THE MESSAGE

*I do not despise genius—indeed,
I wish I had a basketful of it. But yet,
after a great deal of experience and observation,
I have become convinced that industry is a better horse
to ride than genius. It may never carry any person as far as
genius has carried individuals, but industry—patient,
steady, intelligent industry—will carry thousands
into comfort, and even celebrity; and
this it does with absolute certainty.*

WALTER LIPPMANN

American Journalist, Political Writer, and Philosopher

1889-1974

Integrity and Industry

- Be a self-starter. On your job, don't sit idly. Look for what needs to be done and do it. And strive to do it just a little bit better than it has been done before. Add polish to everything you touch.

- Come in fifteen minutes earlier than you are expected at work and stay fifteen minutes longer.

- Be honest. If the cashier gives you too much change, give it back. Instead of downloading songs off the Internet for free, shop reputable Web sites and pay for the ones you want.

- There's no such thing as a "little white lie." Always tell the truth. When the truth will hurt another person, surround it with love and affirmation; be tactful.

- Be a person others can count on. Be responsible and reliable.

- Read how God promises to bless you when you are a person of integrity:
  - He will uphold you (Psalm 41:12).
  - You will walk securely (Proverbs 10:9).
  - Your integrity will guide you (Proverbs 11:3).
  - Righteousness will guard you (Proverbs 13:6).

Integrity needs no rules.

ALBERT CAMUS

Representative of Nonmetropolitan French Literature

1913-1960

Keep your heart with all diligence, for out of it spring the issues of life.

PROVERBS 4:23 NKJV

Heavenly Father,

Graduating isn't an accident—You know how hard I've worked. I plan to apply that same diligence to what lies ahead for me. A clear focus, extra hours, lots of hard work, whatever it takes to succeed.

One thing concerns me though, Lord. I want to be sure that my pursuit of excellence does not cause me to compromise my integrity. I don't ever want to be the kind of person who cuts corners when I'm driving toward a goal.

I need Your guiding hand, Your still, small voice to help me keep things in perspective. When I'm tempted to bend the rules or step on someone or reconfigure the truth, I ask You to keep me walking in integrity. And, Lord, I give You my promise that I will listen and respond. I believe that the rewards of my hard work will taste even sweeter when they are obtained in a way that's pleasing to You.

Amen.

He'll Provide a Way

My husband, Don, and I believe God has a will and a plan for our lives. As our daughters, Diane and Kathryn, were growing up, we always told them, "If God wants you to go to college, He'll provide a way."

Don and I thought God would make provision for them through us. Isn't that the way the Lord is supposed to work—through His people? Who more logical than parents?

But when our daughter Diane was ready for college, my husband had just lost his job during a recession, and I hadn't worked in seventeen years. Writing checks for college seemed out of the question.

Diane had always been drawn to children, especially those who were blind or deaf. Then Ken Medema, a blind musician, visited our church and shared the story of his work in music therapy with the physically, mentally, and emotionally disadvantaged. His words touched Diane's heart, and she felt God was leading her in that direction.

The long weeks of summer passed, and college continued to be out of reach for us financially. Still, our family felt God's assurance that Diane would attend college in the fall.

Only one Oklahoma school offered a degree in music therapy—Phillips University in Enid. Diane applied and received two scholarships, as well as financial assistance through the work-study program.

To pay her way through college, Diane also worked as a theater cashier, taught piano lessons, and directed music classes for blind and deaf children. At a local state hospital, she worked with emotionally disturbed children. Additionally, she found time for involvement in a local church as accompanist, orchestra member, and teacher. God provided a way to make her dreams come true.

God's provision for our younger daughter Kathryn's college education was like a jigsaw puzzle with many pieces making it possible. By that time, Don and I were able to contribute a little and the rest came from scholarships, grants, work-study programs, loans, and even an anonymous gift.

Kathryn was our creative child. She left our home to attend Chapman College in Southern California, majoring in film and theater, and performed as an actor, singer, and dancer. She was also able to spend a semester at King Alfred's College in England. The first undergraduate student at Chapman to ever direct a full-length play, she was nominated for the school's prestigious Cheverton Trophy as outstanding senior student.

When things got tough after graduation, the girls always remembered how God had blessed them. The book of Genesis relates the story of Abraham at Bethel, his journey into Egypt, and his waywardness there. It also tells how God convicted Abraham of his disobedience and doubt and then renewed the blessing as he "went back to Bethel."

Our daughters' college years are long over. Whenever doubt or depression threatened to engulf them, they returned in their memories to their own Bethels. For Diane, it was Phillips University in windswept northwestern Oklahoma, and for Kathryn, the old California city of Orange where Chapman College nestles under the palms.

God always provided above and beyond what we could ever ask or dream for our daughters. They both met Christian husbands in their college locations, and their postgraduate lives have been rich with service.

"If God wants you to go to college, He'll provide a way." Our statement made in faith was true years ago, and its principle still holds today. God provides unfailingly and wondrously for the things He has willed for our lives.[5]

★

Integrity and Industry

God always keeps His word, and because I am His child, created in His image, I choose to be a person of integrity who honors Him. When I say I will do something, I do it. I put in a full day's work and do not steal from my employer by conducting personal business on company time. I will not take things that don't belong to me or cheat in any way. In turn, God promises to bless me: He upholds me, I walk securely, and my integrity guards and guides me.

In matters of principle, stand like a rock;
in matters of taste, swim with the current.

THOMAS JEFFERSON
American President 1801-1809
1743-1826

Work is not primarily a thing one does to live,
but the thing one lives to do. It is, or should be,
the full expression of the worker's faculties,
the thing in which he finds spiritual, mental,
and bodily satisfaction, and the medium in which
he offers himself to God.

DOROTHY L. SAYERS
English Author of Detective Novels
1893-1957

Dedicate some of your life to others. Your
dedication will not be a sacrifice;
it will be an exhilarating experience.

Thomas Dooley

American Physician and Author

1927-1961

Success Is Love and Service

The measure of our success will be the measure of our ability to help others.

F. B. Meyer
British Baptist Preacher
1847-1929

All jobs are service jobs.
Remember that as you leave school,
prepare your résumé, and step out in pursuit
of success and happiness.
Serving others—even in little things—
sweetens everything it touches, your work,
your relationships, your life.

*Each one should use whatever gift
he has received to serve others,
faithfully administering God's grace
in its various forms.*

1 Peter 4:10

The Christian faith is not one of cold intellect;
rather it is full of love, grace, and humanity.
It has the strength and compassion with which
Christ was able to change the course of human life
from evil to good, from selfishness to service,
from despair to faith in the highest.

William T. Manning
Protestant Episcopal Minister
1866-1949

Love and Service

- Give back to your community through acts of service: work in a food bank one morning each month, visit a nursing home, take a meal to a shut-in, volunteer as a Big Sister or Big Brother, teach a child to read.

- Be sensitive to the people in your world and offer an open ear to those who are carrying burdens. Share God's promises and lead them to Him.

- Commit random acts of kindness: give up your place in line, take the newspaper to an elderly neighbor, hold the door open for parents carrying small children, wash a single mother's car, shovel snow for a neighbor who can't, welcome new neighbors to your neighborhood. If it will reflect kindness, do it!

- Give anonymous gifts. This could be as simple as sending an encouraging note or leaving a bag of groceries on the porch of a person in need. Why not pay the tab for a complete stranger in a restaurant?

- In all that you do, remember that you are the only Bible some people will ever read. Let your light shine and represent the goodness of God.

Heavenly Father,

I always thought that serving You meant that I had to become a missionary or a preacher or run some kind of charity for the poor. But now I realize that You have called me to serve You in whatever profession I enter.

Help me to see the opportunities to serve others in my daily work, whatever that might be. As the writer of inspiring books, as the maker of safe and economical consumer products, as a person who is entrusted with enforcing the law, or tending to the sick, help me to do it as a service to You and to others. And, Lord, if You should call me to a life of service without pay, without recognition, I pray that You would give me the courage and the fortitude to look to You for my needs and to work on in my calling, knowing that my work is changing lives for eternity.

Amen.

Things Change

"Why the long face?" I asked my son, Jeric. "It's your graduation day. A few more hours and you'll have your diploma in hand. Aren't you supposed to be happy about that?"

No answer, just a halfhearted smile aimed in my direction.

Jeric had always been a hard person to read. He tended to be shy and introspective, but his current attitude baffled me. His two best buddies were in the other room, laughing and clowning, obviously having a great time, while Jeric couldn't seem to come out from under his own little rain cloud.

"Dad wants to take pictures," I reminded him. "Let's go out by the pool."

The boys stood along the deck railing, offering to throw each other in, cap and gown and all. Each mugged for the camera, arms around shoulders. "Hey, stand still for the picture!" my husband shouted.

I couldn't help remembering these three boisterous boys—it seemed like only a few days earlier—playing in the pool, dunking each other, racing from one end to the other. Bobby and Jeric had been friends since sixth grade and Tyler joined them in the eighth. It was rare to see one without the others. We'd watched them grow up together. Hard to believe they were all going off to college in a few short months.

I watched Jeric as the evening wore on, even commented to his father that something seemed a little off—but I couldn't put my finger on it. Finally, I asked again in the precious few minutes between our after-commencement Mexican food and the all-night, lock-in party at the high school.

"Come on, Mom; it's nothing," he protested. "It's just hard, you know, thinking about how things are going to change. Tyler's going into the Air Force, Bobby's staying here and going to community college, and I'll be leaving for State in August. Everybody says we'll still be close, but I'm pretty sure we won't. It's just tough to know that nothing will ever be the same."

My mind raced, searching to find a solution—but he was right.

"Yes. Things are changing," I offered cautiously. "But some things will stay the same. The way you love each other, for one. Love is pretty versatile. It reinvents itself to accommodate changing circumstances. Your relationship with Dad and me will change, too, but we won't love you any less. Don't be afraid to trust God."

"Hey, Mom, thanks, but I've got to go." He turned to walk off down the sidewalk, but then he unexpectedly turned and came back. He was smiling now—one of his authentic beamers. He gave me a quick hug and said, "I love you," before racing off to his car where Tyler and Bobby were swatting each other with the mortarboards they'd abandoned in the backseat on the way to the restaurant.

"What was that all about?" my husband asked.

"Change is always tough, but love will get him through," I answered. We were both too busy waving to say more.[6]

Love and Service

I am committed to living as Jesus did. I will be accepting of the people I come into contact with and allow God's love for them to flow through me. I show compassion to the hurting, I encourage the brokenhearted, and I extend mercy to those who need it. Instead of being so consumed with the details of my own life, I will take interest in the lives of others and strive to make a difference when I can. Jesus laid down His life for me, so I, too, hope to invest my life to love and serve the people who touch my world.

There's a saying I've heard—most people offer it as a lesson
for living—that life is divided into three phases:
you learn, then you earn, then you serve.
By that yardstick, you've done your learning,
and now it's time to do some earning—
to build the career that allows you
to give back later.

J. C. Watts

One of College Football's Greatest Quarterbacks
and National Politician

Prepare yourself for the world as athletes do for their exercises; oil your mind and your manners to give them the necessary suppleness and flexibility; strength alone will not do.

LORD CHESTERFIELD
English Statesman and Author
1694-1773

Success Is Purpose and Preparation

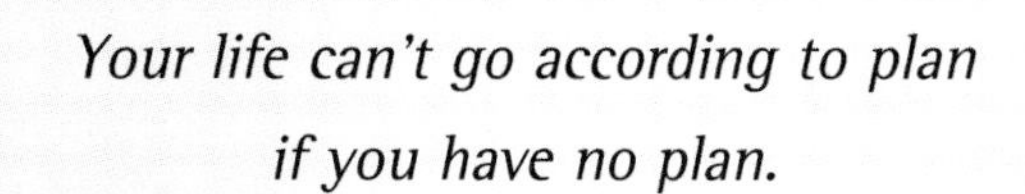

Your life can't go according to plan
if you have no plan.

AUTHOR UNKNOWN

How can you succeed if you don't know
where you're going? Be assured,
God has a wonderful purpose for your life.
The Bible says He established it before He set
the foundations of the earth.
He's eager to help you discover that purpose—
one day at a time. Look to God, and
He'll show you exactly where to begin.

It's in Christ that we find out who we are and what we are living for. Long before we first heard of Christ and got our hopes up, he had his eye on us, had designs on us for glorious living, part of the overall purpose he is working out in everything and everyone.

EPHESIANS 1:11-12 THE MESSAGE

The long span of the bridge of your life is supported by countless cables called habits, attitudes, and desires. What you do in life depends upon what you are and what you want. What you get from life depends upon how much you want it—how much you are willing to work and plan and cooperate and use your resources. The long span of the bridge of your life is supported by countless cables that you are spinning now, and that is why today is such an important day.

Make the cables strong!

L. G. ELLIOTT

Purpose and Preparation

- Work hard to develop your verbal and written skills.
- Learn the importance of such concepts as teamwork, cooperation, respect, trust, caring, love, etc.
- Learn the value of being a positive, enthusiastic person.
- Never quit learning. Regardless of your field of expertise, there's always room to grow. Read books, attend seminars, take additional classes. Determine to be the very best in your field.
- Find a mentor, preferably someone who shares your Christian beliefs. If possible, try to find someone who would be willing to meet with you once a month or even every couple of months. If you don't know someone who fits the bill, perhaps your pastor or another trusted individual does.
- Spend quiet time with the Lord every day, even if it is only a few minutes. Staying connected to Him in prayer and through His Word is essential to staying on target with His ultimate purpose for your life.

The only true happiness comes from squandering ourselves for a purpose.

JOHN MASON BROWN
American Literary Critic
1900-1969

We know that in all things God works for the good of those who love him, who have been called according to his purpose.

ROMANS 8:28

Heavenly Father,

I know You have a wonderful plan for my life—I believe that, I really do! But here I am graduating, and I'm still not sure what it is. I thought I'd know more by now. I honestly thought it would all be mapped out in front of me.

Help me, Lord, to go out from here with the quiet assurance that You will help me take the right step in the right direction at the right time. This must be what it means to live by faith. It's a little unnerving—not like a school course where I know all the assignments and test dates ahead of time. Still ... I am going to take one step at a time, trusting that You will walk alongside, keeping me on track.

Thank You, Father, for giving my life meaning and purpose one day, one step at a time.

Amen.

Joy in the Journey

At thirty-two, Bill was one of the oldest students in his graduating class. Standing on the platform to receive his diploma, his hands were sweating and his heart pounding so hard in his chest he was sure he was having a heart attack.

How had he made it this far? How had he managed to earn a degree in pastoral studies? Who would have thought God could use someone with his background? With only a GED and a history of getting into trouble, not many people would have bet on Bill finishing school.

"You'll never make it, Bill," his mother had said. "No one can change like that."

But he had done it! God had done it. It had been a long three years, tough academically for someone who had wasted his high school years in drinking and rough living. He might not have made straight A's in college, but he had worked hard. He studied during breaks on the job and struggled to stay awake in class after working all night and giving up time with his kids.

Three years ago Bill had packed up his wife, Laurie, and their two sons, one just three months old, and headed for Oklahoma City to attend Heartland Baptist Bible College. It had been a long trip from the heart of Montana. Taking little with them, the family headed out on faith, prayer, and the love of their home church.

"You'll be in our prayers every day," friends shouted as Bill and his family drove out that warm sunny day. It had been rough at first, but they had experienced a lot of joy in the journey.

"God used Bible college to show me how much I needed Him," Laurie said. "And that I didn't know the Lord like I thought I did."

Digging deep into the Bible and learning to share it with others brought Bill and Laurie great joy, as did fellowship with the other married students. They spent evenings together with friends, sharing their food and watching their children play. Everyone would bring what little they had and prepare a feast.

It was amazing to watch God supply their needs even when it seemed there was no way out of the financial trial. Groceries or Christmas gifts for the kids would appear on their doorstep, left by anonymous donors. One time a family at church gave Bill a hundred dollar bill, not even knowing Laurie had just broken her glasses.

"The Lord laid it on my heart to give you this," Brother Smith said. He smiled as he quietly slipped the money into Bill's hand.

What a trouper his wife had been through it all! Laurie

had practically raised the boys alone with Bill being busy with work, school, ministry, and studying. And the greatest blessing of all was the birth of their third son, Justin.

Bill snapped back to the present as he heard his name being called. It was his turn to receive his diploma. Laurie smiled at him from the front row. She was expecting their fourth baby, a little girl. Was it only minutes ago she had hugged him, saying, “I knew you could do it!” She had earned this degree as much as he had.

Bill walked forward proudly and stretched out his hand to accept the diploma. It was time now to go forward and celebrate not only what had been accomplished in the past three years but what was yet to come.[7]

★

Purpose and Preparation

God has had a plan for my life since before the world began, and I am committed to fulfilling it. It is the place of greatest blessing for me. As I discover the gifts and talents God has endowed me with, I will be faithful to develop them. I want to honor God with my life and the gifts He has given me. As His purpose for my life is revealed to me, I will execute it with excellence so that all my ways will glorify Him.

It's the mood and the purpose
at the inception of each day
that are the important facts
in charting your course for the day.
We can always make a fresh start,
no matter what the past has been.

George Matthew Adams
Philosopher
1750-1795

Thankfulness invites God

to bestow a second benefit.

ROBERT HERRICK

American Novelist

1591-1674

Success Is Praise and Thankfulness

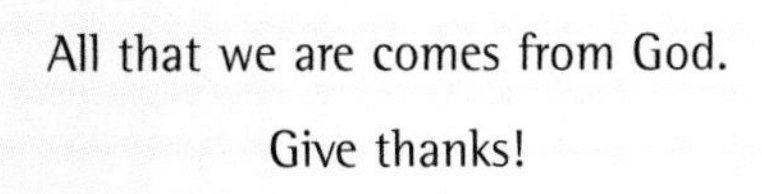

All that we are comes from God.

Give thanks!

AUTHOR UNKNOWN

Success could be described as a tightrope suspended high overhead—one wrong step could take you out of the game. Praise and thankfulness serve as a balance pole. Make a strong start by thanking those people who have helped you reach this day. Wherever the next step takes you, keep both hands on your pole and live a life of gracious appreciation.

Since we are receiving a kingdom that cannot be shaken, let us be thankful, and so worship God acceptably with reverence and awe.

HEBREWS 12:28

I thank You for a daily task to do,
For books that are my ships with golden wings,
For mighty gifts let others offer praise—
I'm thanking You, God, for little things.

Matthias Claudius
1740-1815
German Poet and Theologian

Praise and Thankfulness

- Stay in touch with those who have invested in your life and make it a routine to write, e-mail, or call to express your gratitude. Before too much distance comes between you, get those contact numbers and addresses from the teachers, friends, pastors, coaches—all those who invested in your life.

- Take part in an "anonymous" good deed. This is a demonstration of your thankfulness for what others have done for you. It's also a great way to keep life in perspective by looking outside your own world.

- Spend a few minutes every day praising and thanking God. If you can't think of what to say, turn to the book of Psalms. Its words are timeless and can help you put words to the thoughts and feelings in your heart.

- Keep an ongoing log of the good things God has done for you. Times of discouragement come to everyone, but when they come knocking at your door, whip out your list and reflect on the many times that God has demonstrated His faithfulness to you.

Gratitude unlocks the fullness of life. It turns what we have into enough, and more. It turns denial into acceptance, chaos to order, confusion to clarity. It can turn a meal into a feast, a house into a home, a stranger into a friend. Gratitude makes sense of our past, brings peace for today, and creates a vision for tomorrow.

MELODY BEATTIE
Author and Journalist

HEAVENLY FATHER,

MY HEART IS FULL! I'VE FELT YOUR MIGHTY HAND GUIDING ME EVERY STEP ALONG THE WAY. AND NOW, I CAN STAND UP AND SHOUT THAT WE'VE DONE IT, MADE IT, PULLED IT OFF—YOU AND I! I'LL ALWAYS BE GRATEFUL FOR THE TIMES YOU HELPED ME TO STAY FOCUSED ON MY STUDIES, GAVE ME THAT LITTLE EXTRA SOMETHING I NEEDED TO FINISH EACH TOUGH ASSIGNMENT, KEPT ME ON TARGET WITH MY GOALS AND OBJECTIVES. THIS DIPLOMA BELONGS TO BOTH OF US.

LORD, AS I GO ON TO THE NEXT STEP IN MY LIFE, I'M GOING TO NEED YOUR HELP MORE THAN EVER. I KNOW I CAN COUNT ON YOU. AFTER ALL, YOU HAVE NEVER, EVER LET ME DOWN. RECEIVE MY THANKS FOR ALL YOU'VE DONE AND MY GRATITUDE FOR WHAT YOU WILL DO IN THE YEARS AHEAD. YOU ARE MY ANCHOR!

AMEN.

Displaced Person

When I entered school in America at the age of fourteen, I was classified as a "displaced person." My family and I had lived through World War II in Hungary, followed by four years in a refugee camp, before sailing to the United States. The horrors of the past had taken a toll on my fragile self-esteem.

I was a mousy, shy, "displaced person," who spoke with a thick accent and was barely acknowledged by my American peers. I longed to be just like those beautiful, giggling girls, with swinging ponytails, who passed me every day in the hallways. But my past still haunted me.

I attended an all-girls Catholic school run by nuns, and my classmates came from all over the city. The older girls even drove their own cars. My grandparents and I lived in a small rental house nearby so that I could walk to school. Every morning that I entered those big front doors, I did so with great trepidation, painfully aware of being different.

I knew it was a great sacrifice for my grand-parents to send me there. We were newcomers to America, money was scarce in our household, and the school tuition, uniforms, and books were expensive. But I felt lucky to have been accepted since my English was not perfect.

Despite my language struggles, I managed to pass all my courses that first year and I even made a few friends. What a relief! I spent the summer working part-time at a local dime store and hanging out with my pals at the shores of Lake Erie.

In September, it was time to don the old blue and gold jumper and white blouse and go back to school. I entered the building with the same trepidation and dread, and although some of the girls greeted me cheerily, I had not turned into a swan over the summer. Then I walked into Sister Eleanor's sophomore English class, and soon everything changed for the better.

Sister Eleanor had the bluest eyes, a smile that lit up the whole room, and a gentle, sympathetic manner. She instantly recognized my pain and asked me questions in front of the class about my previous life. She wanted my classmates to better understand why I was different from them. She explained the circumstances and gently encouraged them to put themselves in my shoes and see how they would feel coming to a new country. I quickly concluded that God had blessed me with one of His angels for a teacher. Then the good sister gave us all our first assignment of the new school term.

"I want you all to write an essay of at least four pages about something memorable that has recently happened to you. It will be due a week from today." When we left the classroom, I wasn't too sure what an essay was, but I put my heart and soul into that assignment.

I wrote about being crammed, with hundreds of other immigrants, on a ship taking us to our new country. I wrote about Dave, the young American who worked on that ship, who befriended me and bought me my first Coke. I wrote about the first time I saw the Statue of Liberty and what a thrill that was and about being processed at Ellis Island. I wrote about how it felt to be in a new country, where the language and customs were different. As I wrote, I realized that I loved writing!

The day after we handed in our essays, Sister Eleanor asked me to read mine aloud to the entire class. To my great surprise, my classmates applauded when I finished. Then I was sent to read it throughout the school and got the same reaction. Suddenly, girls surrounded me in the hallway, telling me how much they liked my essay, suggesting that I was a good writer, asking me questions, paying attention to me. With the stroke of my pen, I was no longer a "displaced person"—I was finally a part of the group.

Two years later, when I tossed my cap in the air with the graduating class of 1955, I thought about Sister Eleanor. With her caring, understanding ways, she had cured my culture shock, and I graduated as the confident, young American girl I had longed to become.[8]

Praise and Thankfulness

This is the day that the Lord has made. I rejoice and I am glad in it! I will serve the Lord with gladness and come before His presence with singing. He is the source of all the blessings in my life, so I will magnify and exalt Him about all things. I thank Him for my health, my family, my friends, the privilege of living in a free country, meeting my needs, and the very air that I breathe. I praise Him with my whole heart and glorify His name.

You can learn to give thanks
even if you don't feel particularly thankful.
Thankfulness, like forgiveness,
is not an emotion.
Thankfulness is an intelligent response
of gratitude to God.

ERWIN W. LUTZER
Author and Pastor of Chicago's Moody Church

O Lord! That lends me life.
Lend me a heart replete with thankfulness!

WILLIAM SHAKESPEARE
Greatest Dramatist Ever Known, Finest English-Language Poet and
World's Most Notable Author
1564-1616

Of all the forces that make
for a better world, none is so indispensable,
none so powerful, as hope. Without hope men are
only half alive. With hope they dream and
think and work.

CHARLES SAWYER
American Photographer
1868-1954

Success Is Cheerfulness and Hopefulness

Those I have seen succeed have always been cheerful and hopeful. They went about their business with a smile on their faces.

Charles Kingsley
English Author and Clergyman
1819-1875

Graduation Day is often the time when
the carefree days of youth give way to the
pressures of everyday living.
Daily routines can crush cheerfulness and
pressing responsibilities can censor hope.
But true success—the kind that includes living in
harmony with God's will—clings to hope and good
cheer. They are an integral part of the package.
Without them, there are accomplishments
—but no true successes.

May God grant you your heart's desire, and fulfill all your plans.

PSALM 20:4 NRSV

Make us thy mountaineers.
We would not linger on the lower slope,
Fill us afresh with hope,
O God of hope.

AMY CARMICHAEL
Outstanding Christian Missionary
1867-1951

Cheerfulness and Hopefulness

- Practice seeing the cup half full rather than half empty. In other words, look for the positive in every situation. For every negative thought that crosses your mind, try to think of at least one positive factor to ponder.

- Buy a Bible promise book filled with uplifting scriptures. Choose one that is organized by topic. When you find a scripture that is particularly encouraging for your situation, highlight it, or using an index card or sticky note, write it down and put it where you will see it often.

- Smile! It's amazing how much it will improve your outlook.

- Spread cheer to others. You'll find it coming back to you.

- Never lose heart. Remember, your Father is a miracle worker! Nothing is impossible for Him, and He has filled His Word with example after example of His faithfulness. There's always hope in Him!

Hope looks for the good in people instead of harping on the worst in them. Hope opens doors where despair closes them. Hope discovers what can be done instead of grumbling about what cannot be done. Hope draws its power from a deep trust in God and the basic goodness of mankind. Hope "lights a candle" instead of "cursing the darkness." Hope regards problems, small or large, as opportunities. Hope cherishes no illusions, nor does it yield to cynicism.

FATHER JAMES KELLER

American Priest and Founder of the Christopher Movement

1900-1977

HEAVENLY FATHER,

YOU KNOW THAT I'M NOT ALWAYS THE MOST GLOWINGLY OPTIMISTIC PERSON IN THE ROOM. I CAN SOMETIMES BE INTENSE AND NURSE MY NEGATIVE THOUGHTS AND FEELINGS. I'D LIKE TO CHANGE, BUT I REALLY NEED YOUR HELP.

LORD, HELP ME TO DEVELOP A CHEERFUL DISPOSITION BY CHOOSING AGAIN AND AGAIN AND AGAIN TO LOOK ON THE BRIGHTER SIDE OF THINGS. POINT OUT TO ME THE POSITIVE, THE HUMOROUS, THE HOPEFUL IN THE SITUATIONS I ENCOUNTER AND IN THE PEOPLE I MEET. WHEN I DON'T RESPOND IN A QUICK, POSITIVE MANNER, GIVE ME ONE OF YOUR MEANINGFUL NUDGES. DON'T GIVE UP UNTIL I'VE MOVED TO THE SUNNY SIDE OF THE STREET. I KNOW IT WILL TAKE SOME EFFORT, BUT I'M WILLING TO MAKE THE INVESTMENT, AND I BELIEVE THAT A BETTER, BRIGHTER, HAPPIER FUTURE IS AHEAD.

AMEN.

Reinventing Willie

It was Lily Morgan who first called me Willie. Up until kindergarten, everyone called me Wilhemina, but she discovered that our names rhymed if she called me Willie. So from then on, it was Willie and Lily.

"What's your favorite verse from ... Jeremiah?" Lily shielded her eyes from the late spring sun. We sat on the dock that she and her dad had built at the cattail fringe of their big green pond.

"Stand at the crossroads and look," I answered dreamily, "ask for the ancient paths, ask where the good way is, and walk in it, and you will find rest for your souls."

"Hmm." Lily chewed on the sweet stalk of field grass. "Why that one?"

"I don't know."

"Yes, you do. Why that one?"

I was shy with most people, but Lily made me feel safe. Still, I considered before answering. "It's the crossroads part, I guess. It's like somebody's taking a trip. And they get to a place where they have this big choice to make: should I go this way or that way or take that other road—"

"Or go back," Lily interrupted.

I lay back on the little platform that stuck out over the pond. "I don't think people should go back."

Lily was quiet. We soaked our winter-pale skin in that scrumptious sunshine, not talking in the way that only best friends can.

"You're right," Lily said finally. "Going back is a waste of time. I mean, you've already been there, right?"

I could feel her penetrating look that meant we were about to embark on a "deep meaningful talk." We'd had a lot of those lately, with adulthood reeling us in like a couple of hooked trout. Lily would be leaving in the fall to study physics at Cornell, and thanks to her coaching, I'd landed two free years in a local community college by placing in the top ten of our class.

Lily had big plans for me—way bigger than I had for myself. She said hard work and a positive attitude could accomplish miracles. With God, anything was possible.

What did she know? She had doting parents, a wide-open future, and enough talent and brains to do anything. What did Lily Morgan know about having to resist suffocation by the low expectations of everyone in town? Blakes are all low-life thieves. Blakes never amount to anything.

"It's no use, Lily. I'll never do it. I mean, I appreciate your help and everything, but some people just aren't meant for the good life. You can dress me up as fancy as you please and I'll still be a Blake."

Before my brain registered what was happening, Lily had shoved me over the edge into freezing water up to my neck.

"What..." I sputtered, "...what on earth did you do that for?" I clambered up on the dock, dripping and outraged.

"What's the matter with *me?*" Lily leapt up, her fists clenched. "What's the matter with *you?* Where's your fight?

Do you want to fulfill a bunch of morons' ignorant expectations, or do you want to shoot for something more? So, big deal, you came from a lousy family. Well, boo-hoo-hoo! I feel real sorry for you. Get off your silly duff and change things. Reinvent yourself! It's your life. I thought you had more guts than that!" Lily whipped around and ran toward her house. I could tell she was crying.

Shivering, I made my way home. Something she said wouldn't let me alone: "Reinvent yourself."

I reached my house and considered the ramshackle mess. A few second-hand bikes, shared by all eight of us, were scattered in the yard. A ratty playpen sat crookedly on the rotted porch. My dad's collection of dumpy, old vehicles decorated the yard in white-trash splendor.

Inside the house my mother would be slouched in her greasy recliner, smoking and watching TV soaps with dull eyes. Dad would be home sooner or later—probably later—and then there'd be shouting. I felt the heaviness squelching my little dreams. But Lily's anger had reached inside and smacked me upside the head.

"Reinvent yourself!" Throughout college, her words were my antidote to the hopeless gloom that sometimes crept up on me unexpectedly. I would say them over and over again until I believed that I was somebody.

Then on graduation day, it finally hit me. I was free of my has-been past! Throwing my hat into the air, I laughed with sheer joy. Lily was right! With God's help, anything is possible.[9]

★

Cheerfulness and Hopefulness

Instead of being discouraged or negative today, I am determined to put on a cheerful, hopeful attitude. Instead of being gloomy, I choose to live on the sunny side of life. I can do this because I am God's child and He promises to work everything out for my good. I am never without hope because He is on my side. When negative thoughts or situations present themselves, I will search instead for the positive aspects and focus on them. Because God's Word says that a merry heart does good like a medicine, I choose to stand on His promise and seek the good and positive things in life knowing He will bless my efforts.

You find yourself refreshed
by the presence of cheerful people.
Why not make earnest effort to confer
that pleasure on others?
Half the battle is gained
if you never allow yourself
to say anything gloomy.

Lydia M. Child
American Author
1802-1880

God wants to be loved for Himself and honored for Himself, but that is only part of what He wants. The other part is that He wants us to know that when we have Him, we have everything—we have all the rest.

A.W. Tozer
American Preacher
1897-1963

Success Is Seeking, Knowing, Loving, and Obeying God

Success is neither fame, wealth, nor power;
rather it is seeking, knowing, loving, and obeying God.
If you seek, you will know; if you know, you will love;
if you love, you will obey.

CHARLES MALIK
Lebanese Christian Philosopher and Diplomat
1906-1987

We all want to be successful, to see all our dreams come true. God made us that way so that we would be motivated to become all He created us to be. But too many times people settle for the world's notion of success and end up striving without fulfillment and working without lasting reward. In the end, their potential is wasted. When we place our success in God's hands, He transforms it into something good and pure and eternal. Nothing is wasted; nothing is lost!

Commit to the LORD whatever you do, and your plans will succeed.

PROVERBS 16:3

Walk quietly–
And know that He is God.
Let your life be governed by His guiding hand
E'en though it varies from the way you planned,
Bow your head in sweet submission and
Walk quietly–

AUTHOR UNKNOWN

Seeking, Knowing, Loving, and Obeying God

- Spend the first few minutes of your day reading a chapter in your Bible. The books of John, Psalms, and Proverbs are good choices if you don't know where to begin. A sales associate at a Christian bookstore can help you find a modern translation if you don't already have one.

- Be conscious of God's presence throughout the day. He is with you and in you, everywhere you go.

- Talk to God about your concerns and listen for His answers. Many times those answers will come as persistent thoughts. As you read your Bible, certain verses will speak to your heart. Write down your impressions, and over time you will see answers emerging.

- There are some excellent prayers in the Bible that can help you grow spiritually: Ephesians 1:17-21; 3:14-21; Philippians 1:9-11 (AMP); and Colossians 1:9-12.

- Tell God often how much you love Him.

- Commit to obey Him and do it promptly.

To have faith where you cannot see;
to be willing to work on in the dark;
to be conscious of the fact that,
so long as you strive for the best,
there are better things on the way,
this in itself is success.

KATHERINE LOGAN

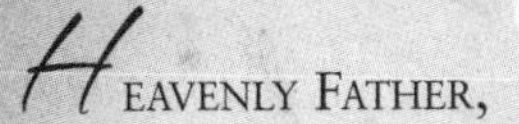

HEAVENLY FATHER,

I KNOW THAT YOU WANT EVERYTHING GOOD IN LIFE FOR ME, AND I WANT TO MAKE A COMMITMENT TO YOU TO GO IN THE DIRECTION YOU LEAD.

KEEP ME CLOSE, LORD. GUIDE ME AND REDIRECT MY PATH THE MOMENT MY FEET TURN IN THE WRONG DIRECTION. GIVE ME WISDOM TO AVOID THE PITFALLS OF SUCCESS SO THAT I CAN WALK A FULLY BLESSED AND RICH LIFE. EQUIP ME WITH THE COURAGE I NEED TO MAKE THE RIGHT CHOICES. TEACH ME TO HEAR YOUR STILL, SMALL VOICE. MY DEEPEST DESIRE IS TO LIVE MY LIFE FOR YOU.

AMEN.

Celebrating God's Will

On the morning of May 11, 1992, I walked in a straight line with my fellow graduates on our way to the chapel where we would receive our diplomas. Around me, students chattered nervously about the future, graduation-party plans, and the recounting of treasured memories between friends. But nothing was as loud as the question I kept asking myself over and over: What have I accomplished?

I'd earned my bachelor's degree in journalism—no doubt about that. I had worked hard, pulled all-nighters, spent time studying instead of goofing off with friends. I had definitely earned that valuable piece of paper. But did I have a plan? Did I know for sure what I wanted to do with my education? The answer was a resounding "No!" No job waited for me. I didn't even have a single contact in my chosen profession. I had a degree. That was it. The rest was up to me, and I had no idea what to do next.

I spent the first year and a half after graduation working in a church. It provided me with some work experience to show myself dependable and gave me a steady income while I searched for jobs. I scoured newspapers from places in the country where I thought I'd like to go. I queried for freelance writing opportuni-ties but quickly discovered that I just didn't have a whole lot to write about yet. I even considered going overseas to South Africa to work for a magazine and was hired to do it if I could come up with the money to get there and get started. *What do I do, God?* was my constant prayer.

I seriously thought about the magazine opportunity, and any other person in my position would have been thrilled with an exciting job in a faraway place. But I wasn't sure about moving to South Africa. I wanted to take the job, but deep down, I knew it was the wrong decision. I just didn't know why. So I continued to seek God's direction. I prayed, I studied my Bible, and I consulted with spiritual mentors whom I trusted, including my pastor.

One day he walked into the office and handed me a book written by a pastor-friend of his about how to know God's will. The book was helpful, but it was my pastor's inscription in the front of the book that rang in my spirit: "Sometimes the Lord's intention in making you wait is to hold you close to Him."

I read those words over and over again. I realized that the future wasn't about my plans. It was about my relationship with God. What was the most important thing to me: God or my plans? Was I looking to God for guidance, or was it to get His approval and rubber-stamp my own plans.

I declined the job in South Africa and stayed at the church until I landed a position at a college working for the public relations director. I delved into graphic design and writing on a freelance basis, giving me the oppor-tunity to put aspects of my education to good use. Then God brought a wonderful man into my life, and I discovered that being a wife and mother was also part of His plan for me.

Where I am now is where God wants me to be. My focus is not on what road to choose next, it's on how I can show my love for God and serve Him where I am today. I definitely had lofty goals and aspirations as a college graduate, as vague as they were. Maybe I didn't know exactly what I wanted to do, but I definitely knew how I wanted to feel—happy, successful, and fulfilled. Ten years after graduation, God has granted me all that and more. Every day is a journey, and I look forward with excitement to what He has in store for me next.[10]

★

Seeking, Knowing, Loving, and Obeying God

I am God's child, and because I am willing and obedient to do His will, He promises that I will be blessed. He's made me to know His voice, and because I follow it, I am not led astray by another. I seek Him and His righteousness before anything else, so everything I need is added to my life. I love Him above all others and am committed to treat the people He brings into my life with care and respect. Surely goodness, blessing, and mercy will follow me all the days of my life.

Better to love God and die unknown than to love the world and be a hero; better to be content with poverty than to die a slave to wealth; better to have taken some risks and lost than to have done nothing and succeeded at it; better to have lost some battles than to have retreated from the war; better to have failed when serving God than to have succeeded when serving the devil. What a tragedy to climb the ladder of success, only to discover that the ladder was leaning against the wrong wall!

ERWIN W. LUTZER

Author and Pastor of Chicago's Moody Church

ENDNOTES

1. Darla Satterfield Davis. Used by permission of the author.
2. Golda Browne, Tulsa, Oklahoma. Used by permission of the author.
3. Joanne Schulte, Santa Ana, California. Used by permission of the author.
4. Rosi Braatz, Lakeville, Minnesota. Used by permission of the author.
5. Trudy Graham, Tulsa, Oklahoma. Used by permission of the author.
6. Rebecca Currington, Tulsa, Oklahoma. Used by permission of the author.
7. Belinda Mooney, Helena, Montana. Used by permission of the author.
8. Renie Burghardt, Doniphan, Missouri. Used by permission of the author.
9. Rhonda Brunea, Cherry Creek, New York. Used by permission of the author.
10. Alison Simpson, Frankfort, Kentucky. Used by permission of the author.

This and other titles in the Celebration Series
are available from your local bookstore.

CelebrateLove
Celebrate Moms
Celebrate Dads

If this book has touched your life,
we would love to hear from you.
Please send your comments to:
editorialdept@whitestonebooks.com
Visit our website at:
www.whitestonebooks.com

"... To him who overcomes I will give some of the hidden manna to eat. And I will give him a white stone, and on the stone a new name written which no one knows except him who receives it."

REVELATION 2:17 NKJV